A GUIDE TO MERSEYSIDE'S INDUSTRIAL PAST

PAUL REE
Illustrations by Duncan Harper

First published 1984   Revised edition 1991

ISBN 0 907768 38 5

Copyright NWSIAH 1991

Published jointly by the North Western Society for Industrial Archaeology and History, Liverpool Museum, William Brown Street, Liverpool, L3 8EN and Countyvise Limited, 1 & 3 Grove Road, Rock Ferry, Birkenhead, Merseyside, L42 3XS. **Printed in England** by Birkenhead Press Ltd., 1 & 3 Grove Road, Rock Ferry, Birkenhead, Merseyside, L42 3XS

FOREWORD

In 1974 a small group of members of the North Western Society for Industrial Archaeology and History came together to make a record of the sites remaining from Merseyside's industrial past. Those were the days when conservation was a dirty word and development was all the rage. The group published its work in a pioneering booklet entitled 'A Guide to the Industrial Heritage of Merseyside'. While the booklet was in production Pilkingtons" Casting Hall, one of St Helens most important monuments, was destroyed by fire. Elsewhere arguments were raging as to the future of the Albert Dock. When a revised edition was produced four years later not a few sites had gone forever.

In 1984 Society members surveyed the County again. The list of sites was updated and additional historical information was added. The booklet's title and format were changed and the first edition of 'Merseyside's Industrial Past' was published jointly with the Birkenhead Press which was making a name for itself in the field of local history. The Merseyside Development Corporation had begun to reclaim derelict dockland and the Albert Dock was being restored. Conservation was becoming an acceptable word and Heritage a marketable asset.

This new revised edition again owes its origins to fieldwork undertaken by Society members. Only a few sites have had to be omitted: many more have been rehabilitated from the derelict to the usable. The Albert Dock thrives, and Birkenhead's Woodside is set to become part of the tourist industry. It is now respectable to have an interest in the industrial past. Can it be that the work of those NWSIAH members sixteen years ago has in some way born fruit?

Paul Rees

CONTENTS

Knowsley	page 1
Liverpool	page 3
St Helens	page 18
Sefton	page 27
Wirral	page 32

The Ordnance Survey Landranger map 108 covers all of Merseyside. Each site is listed with its six figure grid reference and in most cases a street name is also given. The relative importance of each site can usually be gathered from the length of the entry. The entries are classified within the five districts of Merseyside as the Port, Mining and Quarrying, Manufacturing Industries, Transport, Public Utilities and Industrial Housing.

ACKNOWLEDGEMENTS

Thanks are due to Samantha Ball for drawing the maps of the docks, to John Fielding for preparing the artwork and to the National Museums and Galleries on Merseyside for permission to reproduce photographs and illustrations from their collections.

KNOWSLEY

The Borough of Knowsley lies between Liverpool and St. Helens. Since the 1930s, its rural character has been overrun by the urban growth of its neighbours, resulting in the suburban sprawls of Huyton and Kirkby and an untidy rash of bungalows, haulage depots and small-holdings in areas still clinging to their once rural character. The old established town of Prescot had two collieries, three potteries and a 'Cotton Manufactory'. Most importantly, it was the principal U.K. centre for the manufacture of watch movements and clock and watch making tools during the 19th century, when over one hundred small workshops existed mainly in the form of extensions to domestic houses. Its industry is now dominated by the cable works established in 1890.

Thus in this once rural area there are relatively few industrial sites. Many of those that did exist have been overlaid by modern industry and housing.

1. *Watchmaking Factory, Eccleston Street, Prescot.*

MINING AND QUARRYING

CRONTON COLLIERY 475893
Cronton Road (A5080).

Mining began in the area in 17th century. No.1 shaft 242 yards deep closed 1959 and filled 1969. No.2 562 yards, No.3 532 yards sunk 1914-18 by Hulton Colliery Company. Electric winding engines (1920-21) in use when closed February 1984. Connected to L&MR via an extension of Halsnead Colliery branch. Site now levelled and tip reclaimed.

Miners housing at Whiston and Rainhill built by Hulton Colliery in 1925.

MANUFACTURING INDUSTRIES

WATCH FACTORY 472928
Albany Road, Prescot.

A three-storey brick building with impressive large windows. Erected by the Lancashire Watch Company in 1888-9. Watches manufactured until 1910 when the company succumbed to foreign competition. Equipment removed; building became barracks and is currently a Trade Centre. Machinery, products and history at Clock and Watchmaking Museum, Church Street, Prescot.

WATCHMAKING WORKSHOPS 468931
around St. Helens Road, Prescot.

Prescot was the centre for watches, watch parts and small tools manufacture during the 18th and 19th centuries. Many domestic workshops can be identified behind the houses on both sides and off St. Helens Road. Often two-storey brick extensions, they are identifiable by large, many-paned windows. Representative interiors in the Museum, Church Street. Huckle's Factory (468928) at the junction of Eccleston Street and Ackers Street last worked 1965. A free standing 1890 two-storey brick workshop with original windows at rear of 20 Grosvenor Road retains original work benches.

ROAD TRANSPORT

TURNPIKE MILESTONES

A stone milestone on square base inscribed 'Huyton', with curved faces above inscribed 'To Prescot 1 Mile' and 'To Liverpool Exchange 7 Miles' at East Prescot Road, Huyton (449923). Mileposts erected on this turnpike about 1753. Another similar stone at Rainhill Road, Whiston, (378921) now white painted.

TOLL COTTAGE 432906
Roby Road/Station Road, Roby.

White painted brick single-storey cottage. 1750 with later additions. Controlled gate on Huyton loop of Liverpool and Prescot Turnpike Road.

RAIL TRANSPORT

HUYTON STATION 440907
Station Road, Huyton.

Liverpool and Manchester Railway opened 1830, became LNWR 1846. Engineer George Stephenson. This building 1880s when lines quadrupled. Yellow brick offices, waiting room, subway and stationmaster's house, canopy removed. Three L&MR stone sleeper blocks built into lower wall near entrance. Signal box.

ROBY EMBANKMENT 408903-432907
Between Broad Green and Huyton.

Built 1827-29 by L&MR, a massive embankment two miles long and up to 40 feet high, using stone from Olive Mount cutting. Contemporary underbridges e.g. Childwall Lane and Sawpit Lane. Widened 1871.

HALSNEAD COLLIERY BRANCH 452907
Huyton Quarry to Windy Arbor.
South-eastwards.

Early colliery branch connected to L&MR in 1833. Extended to Cronton Colliery in 1918. Stone sleeper blocks in wall at 454906; a walled embankment at 460903. Traces of mining activity and terraced 'pit' houses at site of Halsnead Colliery.

PRESCOT STATION 470922
Station Road, Prescot.

Huyton and St. Helens Railway, 1871. Single-storey common brick building with two-storey stationmaster's house. Hipped slated roof, and canopy.

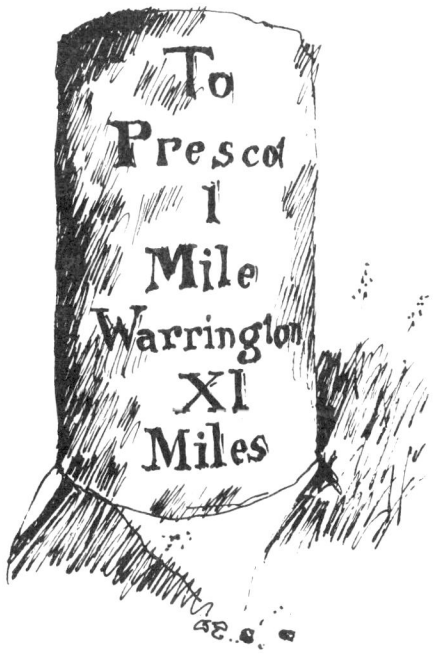

2. *Turnpike Milestone, Whiston.*

LIVERPOOL

Liverpool began as a small fishing, farming and defensive settlement on the eastern shores of the Mersey estuary where an inlet, the Pool, joined the river. It gradually developed as a trading port and, at the beginning of the eighteenth century, the Pool was converted into Britain's first commercial wet dock. Exporting coal and salt in return for sugar and tobacco, the town benefited not only from the expansion of trade with the Americas but also from the industrial growth of its hinterland. During the century, pottery and watchmaking grew to importance as well as the more port related industries such as sugar refining, shipbuilding and ropemaking.

By the end of the century, the town's economy began to change again. There was a rapid extension of the dock system in order to cope with the increased volume of trade, the size of ships and the new steam vessels. Road, river and canal links were improved. The railway appeared and Liverpool became more of a commercial than industrial centre.

As trade grew, so did the population: the districts north and south of the old town close by the docks soon became areas of congested housing and eventually included some of the worst slums in the country. By the early twentieth century, the built-up area formed a semi-circle about three miles in radius. Suburban growth continued, to include the once independent townships of Garston, Walton, West Derby and Wavertree.

Many of Liverpool's industries have moved from the town to outlying new industrial estates. Of the nineteenth century industries which developed on a huge scale to take advantage of the bulk production and distribution facilities offered by the port, only grain remains. Some of the industries which grew up to serve the community, such as food production, continue to do so. The commercial centre of the town is impressive in the scale of its buildings. Above all, however, it is the river, the docks and warehouses which remain as Liverpool's most dominant industrial feature.

THE PORT

LIVERPOOL'S OPERATIONAL DOCKS

Until 1858 the use of the river as a port was controlled by a Dock Committee of the town council, and after that date by the Mersey Docks and Harbour Board. Many of its notable features are by Jesse Hartley, dock engineer from 1824 until 1860. North of the Pier Head the docks are still operational (even if disused as far as Nelson Dock) and permission to visit should be obtained from the Mersey Docks and Harbour Company. They are described in sequence northwards from the Pier Head.

PRINCE'S DOCK   337908

The first dock behind walls opened 1821, built by John Foster. Sandstone dock walls remain unseen behind concrete piling. Transit sheds post 1905. Former passage from George's Dock converted to Graving Dock in 1872-74. Pumphouse on St. Nicholas Place once housed L&MR locomotive Lion. Support columns from former Liverpool Overhead Railway inside dock wall. Half-Tide Dock of 1868 to north. Prince's Jetty adjacent, the second such ferro-concrete structure in country, 1899-1900.

RIVERSIDE STATION   336908
Prince's Parade.

Between Prince's Dock and river was Riverside Station, built 1895 for Atlantic liner passengers and connected via Waterloo and Victoria Tunnels (3,600 yards) to LNWR at Edge Hill. Last used 1971, demolished 1990 apart from small section at south end. Signal box at Steamport Transport Museum, Southport.

WATERLOO DOCK   336912

A single dock of six acres by Jesse Hartley 1834. Totally rebuilt in 1868 as two smaller docks. Six-storey corn warehouse by G.F. Lyster (Hartley's successor as Dock Engineer), 1867, originally one of three,

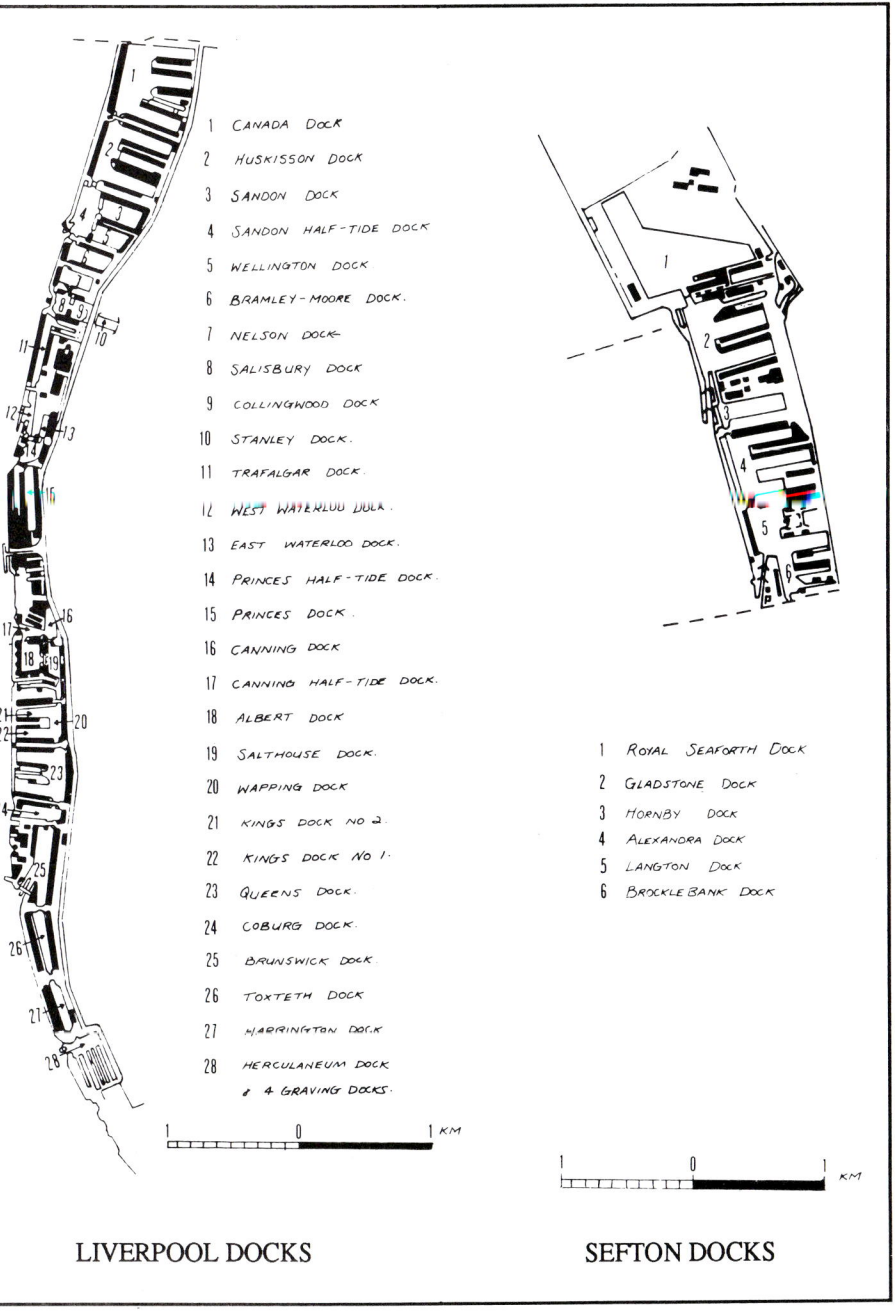

Map of Liverpool and Sefton Docks

the first such with all power-operated handling machinery. Base is a colonnade of square granite pillars supporting stone arches. Brick above. Hoisting machinery enclosed in brick turrets above roof line. Gates in perimeter wall worth noting. Under conversion into flats.

Victoria and Trafalgar Docks to the north, built for steamers 1836. Massively rebuilt 1972.

CLARENCE DOCK   335917

Opened with associated half-tide basin in 1830 for steamships. Filled, but dock outline visible on north side. Dock wall gates of original pattern. Power station built on site in early 1930s, brick hall and three tall concrete chimneys. Disused and partially demolished.

SALISBURY DOCK   334921

Opened with Collingwood, Nelson, Bramley-Moore and Stanley Docks in 1848. River entrance and 'flat 'lock for small river craft typical Jesse Hartley work; cyclopean granite sea wall, cobbled paving to quays. Victoria Bell Tower, hexagonal granite castellated tower with balcony, narrow slit openings and unusual six face clock. Watchman's hut, two-storey oblong building of small irregular stone blocks, battlemented, Tudor style. Dockmaster's house, three-storeys of brick. To north is Nelson Dock.

COLLINGWOOD DOCK   335921

1848, provides access to Stanley Dock under lifting bridge carrying Regent Road. Remains of earlier bridges still visible. Jesse Hartley's granite Dock Wall begins here and runs north to Huskisson Dock. Eighteen feet high, irregular granite blocks; carved plaques name docks. Massive gate posts and turrets at entrances.

STANLEY DOCK   337921

Only dock east of Regent Road. Opened 1848, providing link between dock system and Leeds and Liverpool Canal. Two five-

3. *Victoria Tower, Salisbury Dock.*

storey warehouses by Jesse Hartley, opened 1854. Brick with cast-iron colonnades similar to Albert Dock warehouses. Dock partially filled in 1900, when thirteen-storey red and blue brick Tobacco Warehouses erected between Jesse Hartley's warehouses. Hydraulic pumping station with castellated tower at north west corner. To south west an imposing entrance gate and wall in typical Hartley cyclopean style, with human scale brick office inside.

BRAMLEY-MOORE DOCK   336925

Most southerly of the docks still working. Steamer coaling dock, opened 1848. Part of high level railway viaduct remains, once connected to LYR. Arches beneath formerly housed early refrigerated store of 1884 and 1803 power station for Liverpool Overhead Railway. Red brick accumulator tower dated 1883.

North are Wellington Dock, 1850; Sandon, also 1850 with early (1906) reinforced concrete transit sheds, the first three storey sheds in Liverpool. Sandon Half-Tide 1851.

HUSKISSON DOCK   334933

Opened 1852 as steamer dock with branches of 1861 and 1872. Sugar silo dominates opposite side of dock road.

CANADA DOCK   334949

Opened as timber dock 1858, branch dock with graving docks 1896, on site of timber yard to east. Nearby pubs have appropriate names.

PIER HEAD   337904

Still a focal point for the city. Dominated from north to south by Royal Liver Building, early reinforced concrete, 1910; Cunard Building 1913; Mersey Docks and Harbour Board Offices 1907. All on the site of George's Dock built 1771 enlarged 1820s. Inland the offices and ventilation shaft of the Mersey Road Tunnel, 1930s art deco, with fine decoration and original equipment. Sad 1970s concrete replacement for the 1876 Floating Landing Stage built for Atlantic liners and Mersey ferries.

LIVERPOOL WATERFRONT

To the south of the Pier Head the old dock system is being reclaimed and made available for reuse by the Merseyside Development Corporation. Access is restricted to certain areas. The docks are described in sequence southwards from Pier Head.

OLD DOCK   344900

Liverpool's first dock opened 1715, built by Thomas Steers. Closed 1826 and filled. Customs House by John Foster Jnr. built on site, bombed 1941 and demolished. Present concrete and glass Steers House occupies site, inland of Canning Dock across the dock road.

CANNING DOCK   341910

Formerly outer basin for Old Dock. Converted into Canning Dock 1829. To north part of former St George's Passage remains. Graving Docks 1769, two superb examples of traditional masonry engineering. Stepped side walls and round ends, probably by Henry Berry, then the Liverpool dock engineer. Rebuilt 1815 and 1844. Cast-iron pitch boilers 'Phoenix Foundry' 1811.

Canning Half-Tide 1844, built as entrance to Albert Dock. Single modern gate replaces original pair of wooden mitre gates. Octagonal granite huts for gateman at riverside by Jesse Hartley.

Three-storey red brick and terracotta 1883 Pilotage Office. Liverpool Pilotage Service, second oldest in country. Low brick shed, formerly Liverpool and Glasgow Salvage Company store. All now preserved as part of Maritime Museum.

MANCHESTER DOCK 339901

Manchester Basin 1785, converted to a dock 1818 used for river craft. Filled with spoil from Mersey road tunnel, 1928-36, and now Maritime Museum car park. Adjacent non-rail connected 1890s GWR goods shed was serviced by barges from Birkenhead. Closed 1960, derelict, rehabilitated 1990 as museum accommodation.

SALTHOUSE DOCK 343898

Liverpool's oldest surviving dock of 1753, enlarged 1855 and linked to Wapping. Gable end of Jesse Hartley granite transit shed remains. On site of earlier saltworks. To the south, adjacent to Albert Dock car park, the Duke's Dock of 1773, former property of Duke of Bridgewater, and built to accommodate barges using his canal.

ALBERT DOCK 340897

Opened 1846, on site of shipbuilding yards. Designed by Jesse Hartley, Liverpool's first enclosed dock system. An almost square basin of over seven acres surrounded by five-storey warehouses. Brick construction throughout, floors on shallow vaults between cast-iron beams on cast-iron columns, tensioned by wrought iron rods. Arched roof iron plates resting on wrought iron trusses. At quayside, a colonnade with cast-iron columns supporting brick arches on iron lintels and four upper storeys. Closed as a dock in 1972 and abandoned. Now shops, offices, flats, Tate Gallery and Maritime Museum.

Dock Traffic Office at north-east built 1846-7; architect Philip Hardwick, co-designer of earlier and similar St Katherine Dock, London, and Hartley's consultant on the warehouses. Brick with giant classical portico of cast-iron, now Granada News Studio. Office and warehouses are listed Grade One buildings. Adjacent, the associated hydraulic power station and chimney, built in 1879, now a pub. At north-west, the Piermaster's house, office and cooperage, restored as part of Maritime Museum.

4 *Hydraulic Tower and Gatekeeper's Lodge, Wapping Dock*

WAPPING DOCK   344893

Opened 1855 to link Salthouse Dock with those to the south. Jesse Hartley. Warehouse to east opened 1856. Cellar vaults and five floors of brick, similar to Albert and Stanley warehouses. Now flats. In dock wall at south-east a conical gatekeeper's lodge of granite. Nearby castellated octagonal hydraulic tower dated 1856. Opposite, the refurbished Baltic Fleet public house, typical of such dockland establishments.

KING'S DOCK   342893

Opened 1788, later rebuilt as branches to Wapping. Now the Albert Dock car park.

QUEEN'S DOCK   345890

Opened 1796 and enlarged 1816. Rebuilt and deepened 1856 with basin turned into a half-tide dock. Early 20th century rebuilding turned half-tide dock and adjacent shipyards into two branch docks.

COBURG DOCK   345887

Union Half-tide Dock and Brunswick Basin opened 1816-17. The basin given gates and opened as Coburg Dock for paddle steamers in 1840. Union and Coburg extended and united in 1858. River entrance closed off during 1905 building works. To south a small tidal basin with a slip opened by 1820. Known as the South Ferry basin or the 'Cockle 'Ole', it was latterly the base for the remnants of Liverpool's fishing fleet. Dockyard further south provided all traditional services, smith, foundry, etc from 1842 to 1969. All original buildings demolished 1982.

BRUNSWICK DOCK   346885

A timber trade dock, opened 1832 with half-tide basin (now filled) to west on site of tide mill reservoir. Graving docks to south. Branch barge dock on east side opened 1878. Adjacent shipbuilding yard, graving docks, and barge dock swept away in extensive 1905 rebuilding and opening of new river entrance. Hydraulic power engine house with ornamental accumulator tower and Customs House to south-east, 1889.

TOXTETH DOCK   349879

Opened 1841 for coastal craft. Used for timber trade until Canada Dock opened in 1858, then little used. Totally rebuilt and enlarged by G.F.Lyster in 1888 with the first two storey transit sheds in the port now used as office units.

Harrington Dock to south opened 1839. Rebuilt by Lyster 1883, now filled. Both docks appropriated for use by cargo liner companies after 1880s rebuilding.

HERCULANEUM DOCK   355873

Opened 1866. Enlarged with branch dock and oil jetty in 1881. Filled and redeveloped in 1970s. River gates in situ. Also visible, excavated in 1881 from cliff-face to south and east of dock are sixty magazines, "casemates", for storage of petrol. Each 50 feet deep, 20 feet wide and 19 feet high with iron door for safety, capable of holding 1,000 barrels. Replaced by five early bulk petrol storage tanks on land to south removed during the 1970s.

GARSTON DOCKS   397841

The Old Dock built in 1853 by the St. Helens Canal and Railway Co. to provide outlet for coal. LNWR, LMS and British Transport Dock Board ownership followed. North Dock opened 1876, Stalbridge Dock to the south in 1909. Coal drops now demolished, only the hydraulic pumping station remains. Note that many local pubs are Greenalls: Peter Greenall was chairman of St. Helens Canal and Railway Company!

HALE CLIFF WHARF   450820
Dungeon Lane, Speke.

17th century sandstone and brick quay wall. Refined salt shipped to Cornwall, china clay brought in. Saltworks adjacent from 1697 to mid-1840s. Inclined plane and brick chambers presumed to link with

5. *GWR shed, Manchester Dock, about 1920*

6. *Opening of the Albert Dock, 1846.*

refinery. Site later used for concrete and explosives production and ship breaking. Site currently under investigation by NWSIAH. Nearby pre-19th century cottages, agricultural chapel and customs and excise accommodation.

SHIP STORE MERCHANTS 346899
Hanover Street/Paradise Street.

Former offices and warehouses of Ellis and Co., ship store merchants, sailmakers etc. Now Brimleys and Company. Fine 1890s piece, little altered. Four-storeys, curved frontage of pressed brick, arcaded windows, chimneys and turrets in pediment, low slate roof. Warehouse hoist, and adjacent warehouse dated 1866 in Argyle Street.

WAREHOUSES 346898
around Argyle Street.

MANWEB building in arcaded pressed brick; Hanover Buildings, four-storeys in yellow brick with warehouse of 1876 adjacent; Duttons, a nondescript Liverpool style warehouse in common brick; and Ayrton Saunders and Company overshadowing all in pressed brick and glass. Other mid 19th century examples in an interesting area only three minutes from shops.

WAREHOUSES 345904
Button Street, Mathew Street, Rainford Gardens, Temple Court etc.

Tall brick warehouses, offices and other buildings line a group of short narrow streets. Mostly mid-19th century. Victoria Street cut through the area in 1860s. A commercial area of great character, formerly the centre of the provision and fruit trades and close to the city's shopping area. Much recent rehabilitation.

STANLEY BONDED TEA WAREHOUSE
338920
Great Howard Street/Dublin Street.

Massive rectangular block of 1880s, six storeys of brick, recessed loading bays and small windows. Other examples of 19th century warehousing in Bentinck Street, Grundy Street, Luton Street, Sandhills Lane to the north. Much recent demolition.

WAREHOUSES 348892
Jamaica Street/Watkinson Street.

Remnants of most extensive warehousing area in city. Despite recent demolition some fine examples survive. Mainly late 19th century. Impressive brick six-storey block on Parliament Street. Watkinson Street has warehouses both sides. Compare also Blundell Street and Bridgewater Street.

MINING AND QUARRYING

WOOLTON QUARRY 421870
Church Road, Woolton.

Worked until late 1970s to provide sandstone for Anglican Cathedral.

MANUFACTURING INDUSTRIES

SOUTH END FLOUR MILLS 355880
Grain Street, off Mill Street, Toxteth.

A former windmill site on the sandstone ridge which runs parallel to the river. Wilson King are still milling; the buildings are mostly modern.

HEAP'S RICE MILL 345897
Carpenter Row.

Six-storey plain brick building. Some pre-1843 (Liverpool Fire Act) timber frame construction. Associated seven-storey warehouse.

HIGSON'S BREWERY 350889
Stanhope Street.

Built between 1896 and 1902 by Robert Cain and Sons. Fine example of Victorian tower brewery. Architect James Redford. Built of pressed brick in four phases; five-storeys, clerestories and combined chimney-tower. Excellent terracotta decoration of beer casks, hops, barley etc. Closed 1990 and future uncertain. Modern extensions.

MINERAL WATER FACTORY 350915
Dalrymple Street, off Great Homer Street.

Schofield Brothers' model factory of about 1880. Red brick and terracotta.

MATCH FACTORY 411841
Speke Road, Garston.

Built 1919, an early example of modern functional factory design. Concrete frame and tile decoration. Originally owned by Maguire, Paterson & Palmer Ltd., now Bryant & May. Architects, Mewes and Davis.

TOBACCO FACTORY 367916
Boundary Lane, off West Derby Road.

Large pipe-tobacco factory fronted by distinctive office building in red brick and white stone, with clock tower. Probably 1902, when Ogden's, the present owners, became part of the Imperial Tobacco Company, and moved from Cornwallis Street in the city centre.

TEXTILE MILL 368985
Ormskirk Road, Aintree.

Courtaulds textile mill opened 1930 as part of campaign to diversify Liverpool's economy. Generally expanded 1950-60s, closed 1980, now small industrial estate. 1930 weaving shed, partially demolished. Opposite, Panther Tyres, former farm building from Aintree's agricultural past. Thomas Dolan Engineers in former Smith Crisps Depot, typical 1930s building. Closed railway bridge to sidings.

TANNERY 401838
King Street/Vulcan Street, Garston.

Garston Tanning Company, established 1899. Extensive works, partly disused and demolished 1989. King Street building dated 1911 has slatted upper storeys typical of tanning premises. A private well is still in use; a wide range of leather materials still produced.

KNOTTY ASH BREWERY 40591
East Prescot Road.

Just west of village. A small brewery built in part in 1884 by Joseph Jones & Company, who were taken over by Higsons in 1927. Now shopfitter and builders.

7. *Knotty Ash Brewery.*

ROAD TRANSPORT

MERSEY ROAD TUNNEL   347907
Old Haymarket.

Constructed 1925 to 1934. Engineers Sir Basil Mott and J.M.Brodie. Length 2.13 miles. Under-river section a tube 44 feet in diameter; cast-iron segments held to surrounding rock by concrete grouting. Entrance portal and associated buildings by H.J. Rowse in art deco style. Branch entrance at New Quay (339905) with twin-towered brick ventilation station above. Stone ventilation station at North John Street (342903). Main ventilation station and offices in stone at Mann Island (340901) with good detailing. Original fans and other equipment inside with much original decoration.

LAMB HOTEL   391894
High Street, Wavertree.

Liverpool's best surviving coaching inn, late 18th century. Interesting dolphin street lamps round nearby clock tower.

HORSE TRAM SHED AND OMNIBUS DEPOT   368894
Beaumont Street.

Built 1875 by Liverpool Tramways and Omnibus Company. Stables.

TRAMCAR SHED   390885
Smithdown Road.

Former Liverpool Corporation Tramways shed. New doors but original facade. 1901, now Merseybus. Another shed at junction of Green Lane and Prescot Road of same date. Damaged by fire 1947, now unused. (390913).

TRAMWAY WORKS AND DEPOT
    379906
Edge Lane.

Extensive works built in 1926 to maintain tramcar fleet. Typical works/factory architecture of period. Some track remains. Used as Merseybus depot. Headquarters building in Hatton Garden (345908) 1906 has track in its precinct to allow entrance of cash vans and tower wagons.

CANAL TRANSPORT

LEEDS AND LIVERPOOL CANAL

Liverpool and Wigan section opened in 1770s and through to Leeds in 1816. Now filled south of Burlington Street. Original terminal basin was part of Old Hall Street, south of Leeds Street. From about 1800, another basin west of Old Hall Street. Brick cottages opposite Old Leeds Street (339909) were associated, one being offices of Wigan Coal and Iron Company.

No direct connection to Mersey until 1846, when branch was cut to Stanley Dock. Four locks (not easily accessible) with unusual random-masonry chambers and differing types of paddle gear. Three-storey warehouse in Bankhall Street (343938) built over arm of canal. At 342939, west of Syren Street, are remains of Parkes' boatbuilders yard.

RAIL TRANSPORT

The world's first real railway opened in 1830 between Liverpool and Manchester. Built by George Stephenson and using locomotives, the successors of 'Rocket' at the Rainhill Trials, the line overwhelmed its promoters with passenger traffic. In 1837, rail communication reached London via the Grand Junction Railway; in 1845, the L&MR became part of the London and North Western Railway.

The Lancashire and Yorkshire reached Exchange Station (Tithebarn Street) in 1848; the East Lancashire reached the same station in 1849. The Liverpool, Crosby and Southport line was built to open up the villages along the coast. It also used Exchange and opened throughout in 1850.

The Cheshire Lines Committee reached its Brunswick Dock Station in 1864 and Central Station in 1874. Few traces of either remain.

LIME STREET STATION   351905
Lime Street.

Liverpool and Manchester Railway, opened 1836, connected to original line at Edge Hill by tunnel, east end of which remains, rest opened up into cutting in 1880s. No trace exists of John Foster's 1836 building: part of north wall of Sir William Tite's 1846 building visible along with columns of Hotham St. bridge. Present station by William Baker and Francis Stevenson. North trainshed a 219 feet crescent span of trussed iron and glass on Doric columns, 1869. Southern of 184 feet, 1874. Fronting Lime Street, the London and North Western Hotel, 1871, by Alfred Waterhouse. French Renaissance, with roof full of dormers, chimneys and turrets. Hotel cleaned 1970s, station interior remodelled 1984. L&MR locomotive 'Lion' of 1838 in care of Liverpool Museum.

EDGE HILL STATION   371899
Tunnel Road, Edge Hill.

Opened 1836. Pair of dressed stone two-storey blocks in classical style with pediment and shallow slate roofs. Original rope-winding enginehouses at east end, remodelled for passenger use 1870s. Outer platforms 1880s. Station returned to 1830s appearance in 1980 and is one of oldest still in use. To north, a massive brick stationary engine house for 1849 Waterloo Tunnel rope haulage system.

North of station is disused LNWR fruit and vegetable depot, to the east, the site of LNWR 'Gridiron' marshalling yard; both of 1880s.

8. *Edge Hill Station, 1836.*

CROWN STREET STATION 364898

Original 1830 passenger terminus of L&MR. Became coal yard 1836, disused 1960s. Nothing survived landscaping in 1980, except red 9 brick 40 feet high Wapping Tunnel ventilation shaft of 1890s. Remains of 1830 rope-winding engine station for Wapping Tunnel in cutting under Chatsworth Street (367898).

Wapping and Crown Street tunnel mouths, boiler houses, locomotive sheds, stores, staff accommodation, staircase and chimney bases visible in sides of cutting. 'Moorish Arch' and rope haulage systems excavated by NWSIAH during 1977-80.

EXCHANGE STATION 340907
Tithebarn Street.

Lancashire and Yorkshire Railway terminus of 1884-6 replacing 1848 original. Only the hotel facade fronting Tithebarn Street remains; of stone with attractive iron porch; architect Henry Shelmerdine. Refurbished 1988. Sections of brick viaduct run-ning north from the station still visible. Suburban stations on LYR are undistinguished late 19th century brick, or modern 'bus' shelters.

CRESSINGTON PARK STATION 394850
Knowsley Road, Aigburth.

Cheshire Lines Committee 1864. Closed 1972, restored, electrified and reopened 1978. Brick built, with half-hipped gabled roof. Booking office and stationmaster's house at road level, platforms in cutting. Modern overbridge and awnings. Midland Railway lamp posts. Much typical CLC detail.

HUNT'S CROSS STATION 431851
Speke Road, Hunt's Cross.

.CLC 1879. Four-storeys brick built. Platforms in cutting reached by stairs down from first floor balcony. Much CLC detail, especially barge-boards. Electrified 1983. Compare Aigburth (344050) or St Michael's (366870).

VIADUCT 366962
Sefton Road, off Rice Lane.

Isolated six-arch stone-faced viaduct at Fazakerley North Junction. CLC Southport Extension Railway 1864, carrying tracks over LYR.

9 *Chatsworth Street Cutting, 1980*

GOODS DEPOT 346905
Victoria Street/Crosshall Street/Whitechapel

City centre Midland Railway receiving warehouse. Date-stone 1874. Brick with sandstone detail. Carved names of major towns served. Impressive concave frontage to Crosshall Street. A car park.

PUMPING STATION 340901
Mann Island, Pier Head.

Tall brick building, once housing steam pumps for clearing water from Mersey Railway tunnel. Opened 1886, cleaned 1990. Similar design to its Birkenhead counterpart at Shore Road. Now houses electric pumps.

TUNNEL ENTRANCE 355874
Herculaneum Dock.

Sole substantial relic of Liverpool Overhead Railway, now isolated halfway up cliff-face to north of dock. LOR opened 1893, linking docks between Alexandra and Herculaneum. Extended northwards to Seaforth Sands in 1894 and southwards in 1896 through this half-mile tunnel to an underground station at Park Road, Dingle. Steel decking supported by iron columns 16 feet tall carried two lines and an intensive service of electric trains. Rusted and closed 1956. Platforms of Dingle Station still accessible. Coach No. 3 in care of Liverpool Museum.

AIR TRANSPORT

AIRPORT BUILDINGS 414807
Speke Road, Speke.

Terminal building and control tower of classic pre-war design, 1936-39. Oldest U.K. air transport building in use when closed in 1980s. No. 1 hangar used for aircraft; No. 2 converted to International Terminal. At Banks Lane (409835) is No. 50 hangar, erected 1933 around outbuildings of demolished Chapel House Farm which provided terminal buildings and control tower from 1933 to 1939.

10 *Airport Control Tower, Speke.*

PUBLIC UTILITIES

EVERTON WATERWORKS 361918
Margaret Street, Everton.

Gigantic water tower, 90 feet high, with cast-iron circular tank supported on stone arches of Italianate engine house. Covered reservoir adjacent. Completed 1857; architect Thomas Duncan, the Corporation's first water engineer.

TOXTETH RESERVOIR 359881
High Park Street, Toxteth.

Stone retaining walls about 18 feet high. Round tower at one corner, 1855.

GAS HOLDERS 405844
Speke Road, Garston.

Only remains of extensive Garston Gas Works. Large holder of 4 million cubic feet erected 1893, smaller of 2.25 million cubic feet erected 1925. Used for natural gas distribution.

TELEPHONE EXCHANGE 382892
Lawrence Road/Gainsborough Road, Wavertree.

Built in 1909 by National Telephone Company for Wavertree area. Renamed Sefton Park, superseded by automatic exchange nearby in 1959. Red Ruabon brick, Woolton stone and plinth of Penmaenmawr granite. Now B.T. Engineering Centre.

TELEPHONE EXCHANGE 343902
South John Street/Cable Street.

Four storey brick building erected 1909 as Bank exchange. Burned out 1941, restored as Telegraph House, currently disused.

PILLAR BOXES

'Liverpool Specials' of unique 1863 design, cylindrical, cast-iron surmounted by crown, retained at Sorting Office in Skelhorne Street (352905) and at SE corner of Albert Dock (342897). Penfold hexagonal box in Abercromby Square, 359899.

11 *"Penfold" Pillar Box, Abercromby Square.*

16

CONSTRUCTIONAL CAST-IRON

Liverpool foundries produced much cast-iron ware for architecture as well as street furniture. Phoenix Foundry 1758, and many more by 19th century. St. James Church, 1775, (353891) earliest using cast-iron galley pillars. John Cragg had patented use of cast-iron frames bearing slate slab walls finished to resemble stone by 1813. Window traceries, pillars, roof trusses, bench-ends mass produced in iron and used in St. George's Church, Everton (355925) and St. Michael-in-the-Hamlet (368871) 1812-1815. Architect Thomas Rickman developed the technique especially in the Midlands.

Francis Morton and Company, Garston, exported tin tabernacles and other prefabricated buildings throughout the world. Cast-iron was used for sills, doors, frames, bollards and construction of many warehouses, including the Albert Dock, after the 1843 Liverpool Building Act.

Fine work in the Albany, Old Hall Street, 341907, 1856. First example of cast-iron cantilevered clad construction at Oriel Chambers, Water Street, 341904, by Peter Ellis, 1864. Octagonal Palm House in Sefton Park, 379876.

INDUSTRIAL HOUSING

HARTLEY'S VILLAGE 368965
Long Lane, Aintree.

About fifty neat brick terraced and semi-detached houses with gardens, built by William Hartley for his jam factory workers in 1888. Architect, William Sugden of Leek. Factory mostly demolished.

ELDON GROVE. 346916
off Limekiln Lane.

Rare example of early council tenement block. Brick with half timbered gables. Less gaunt than many other tenements of that period (1911). Converted by a Housing Association for student use.

DUKE'S TERRACE 351898
Behind No. 175 Duke Street.

Reached through covered passage from Duke Street. Last surviving back to back housing in Liverpool; four-storey block (including cellars and attics) with nine front doors on each side. Court in which it stands surrounded by high walls and inaccessible to vehicles. Built about 1850, later converted to nine single dwellings. Currently inaccessible. No. 175 is in poor condition; future uncertain.

ST. HELENS

The remains of early industry are scattered throughout the town, often incorporated into modern industrial sites. The social fabric of the town is shot through with industrial links, as are many of the smaller places recently added to the old St. Helens.

Today, St. Helens means glass, but this was not always so. In the last century, glass was just one industry. Chemicals were almost as important as they were at Widnes. There were over thirty collieries and iron founding and non-ferrous metals had a place as well.

The remains of these 19th century "giants" are becoming hard to find. In the glass industry, changing technology has swept much away. The remains from other industries have been cleared for new estates or open land. The search, therefore, for relics of many a famous concern is tantalising - a piece of wall here, a pair of gate-posts there, glass waste somewhere else. For those who like exploring, the following areas are probably the most rewarding; Ravenhead, Eccleston Street/Boundary Road, Pocket Nook, Sutton, Newton-le-Willows, Billinge Hill and part of Eccleston near the Rugby Ground.

MINING AND QUARRYING

SUTTON MANOR COLLIERY   518908
Jubit's Lane, A568.

Three shafts sunk 1906 to 1914. Nos. 1 & 2 deepened 1952-57 to 2506 feet and 2481 feet. Sinking of No. 3 stopped at 180 feet by First World War and filled. No.1 shaft converted from steam to electrical winding in 1986 with new girder headgear, engine house, fan and compressors. Skip winding. Former steam winder by Fazer Chalmers, Frith, Kent, 1906, exported to Australia; steam air compressor, 1912, to Chatterley Whitefield Mining Museum; steam standby fan engine, 1910, to Wigan Pier.

No 2. shaft is last in an English colliery to be winding under steam. Engine 1914 by Yates & Thom of Blackburn. Lattice headgear.

Adjacent is a typical pit settlement.

BOLD COLLIERY   548935
Bold Lane, Sutton.

Worked 1876 to 1986. Three shafts capped and part of site levelled. Remaining buildings in use as business centre. Spoil heap.

LEA GREEN COLLIERY   505921
Lowfield Lane, Sutton Heath.

Worked 1877 to 1964. Some of remaining buildings used as transport depot. Spoil heap being reclaimed.

RAVENHEAD COLLIERY   502942
Burtonhead Road.

Worked 1866 to 1968. First used Anderton Shearer loader. Shafts nos 10 & 11 capped. Majority of buildings still remain for motor vehicle repairs, light engineering and concrete products.

OLD BOSTON COLLIERY   573976
Haydock, north of A580.

Worked 1868 to 1952. Closed due to underground fire. From 1952 to 1988 was area training centre for NCB. Site levelled 1989 although spoil heaps remain.

PEWFALL COLLIERY   553984

Worked 1860 to 1911. Shafts capped and fenced.

ECCLESTON HALL COLLIERY   457948
Gillars Green, Eccleston.

Capped shafts and spoil heap.

CLOCKFACE COLLIERY 536917
Gorsey Lane.

Worked 1904 to 1966. Three shafts and some buildings remain in use by pigment dispersion and machinery merchants. Spoil heaps.

SHERDLEY COLLIERY 517940

Worked until 1943. Two capped shafts. Site levelled apart from magazine. Spoil heap.

LYME COLLIERY 575965

Worked 1878 to 1964. Three capped shafts, site levelled and fenced. Spoil heap.

SOUTHPORT COLLIERY 545956

Worked 1893 to 1937. Parr shafts Nos. 4 & 5. Fenced off and site reclaimed.

HAVANNAH COLLIERY 548954

Worked 1871 to 1926. Parr shafts Nos. 1, 2 & 3. Site partially reclaimed.

COLLINS GREEN 555943
Fleet Lane.

After closure used as pumping pit for Bold until 1986. Shafts capped. Spoil heap being reclaimed.

PRINCESS COLLIERY 555972

Worked 1892 to 1920. Spoil heap being reclaimed.

SUTTON HEATH 504928
Elton Head Road.

Open cast mining on site since 1988. Of nine shafts, brick headgear of No.1 remains.

ALEXANDER COLLIERY 502942

Two capped shafts and spoil heap.

COKE OVENS 520010 and
Billing Hill. 522017

Site of early 19th century coke ovens, now marked by shale deposits on west side of hill.

QUARRIES

Remains of 18th and 19th century quarrying activity in the Rainhill area (490906) in Mill Lane, View Road and St. James' Road. In St. Helens, there are remains at Thatto Heath Park (497937), Eccleston Hill (488942) and Taylor Park (502949). Also Hard Lane (504970) and Red Row Quarry (575944) on banks of Sankey Navigation. Late 18th century quarry at Billinge Hill (526015) being infilled with domestic refuse.

SAND QUARRY 491989
Berrington's Lane, Rainford.

A source of raw material for Pilkingtons glass works until 1981. Sand moved by rail to the Sand Washery (Sandwash Close, 489999) where iron compounds were washed out. Now Royden Engineering.

MANUFACTURING INDUSTRIES

BRICK, TILE AND POTTERY MANUFACTURE

Some buildings of the Ravenhead Brickworks, Burtonhead Road (512945) survive under different ownership. The Eccleston Brick and Tile Works, Clay Lane (471954) made drainpipes for the Knowsley Estates until about 1936. Its chimney stacks and building are now incorporated in a farm.

At Rainford, the site of the Cat Lane Works (507006) is marked by many fragments of broken pipe. A large chimney marks the use of Rookery Farmstead (487001) as a pottery, possibly since 1780.

RAINFORD POTTERY 491996
Mill Lane, Rainford.

Survives 1964 closure as a series of single-storey brick buildings and a short chimney. Tramway runs south-west for 1,200 yards to claypit at 486986. Related building known as Dial House behind houses adjacent to Bottle and Glass Inn at 487987. Also adjacent a single-storey cement rendered brick building, now MLR, formerly a clay pipe factory, excavated by Liverpool University.

RAVENHEAD GLASS BOTTLE WORK
515947
Warrington Road, St. Helens.

Opened by Nuttall and Company, 1840s, amalgamated with Carrington-Shaw and Company, 1850s. Now United Glass Sherdley Works. At rear of site, visible from Watson Street is former No. 7 bottle making shop. Constructed about 1886 with a Siemens tank furnace heated by producer gas. Working end of furnace was at apsidal end of building, where arches were open and tarpaulin used to keep out bad weather. Oval cone protrudes through roof to carry waste heat away from work, supported on cast pillars and beams. In basement two pairs of air and gas flues survive. Building became a store in 1918. Nearby Power House contains variety of antiquated electric air compressors. Little else survived 1982 site clearance.

RAVENHEAD GLASS WORKS
502945
Prescot Road, St. Helens.

Pilkingtons Fibreglass Plant and Head Office, modern. Also excellent Glass Museum. Production began at Thatto Heath about 1696 and in Prescot in 1721 British Plate Glass Company set up at Ravenhead 1773-77. Pilkingtons took over late 19th century. Historic 1773 casting hall destroyed by fire in 1970s.

12 *No 7 Bottle Shop, Ravenhead Glassworks.*

CROWN GLASS WORKS 510950
South of Chalon Way, St. Helens.

Now Pilkingtons Sheet Glass Works. Good view of site from multi-storey Precinct car park. Site of Pilkingtons first window (crown) glass furnace (1830) marked by plaque on corner of Watson Street. Present buildings are post 1876. Former head office in Grove Street. Adjacent to canal the remains of a glass cone, protruding through hipped roof building. Built 1883, the cone is a roof vent supported on cast-iron columns over former Siemens reverberatory tank furnace.

SUTTON OAK GLASSWORKS 530937
Lancots Lane, Sutton.

Built 1837 for Manchester and Liverpool Plate Glass Company. Fragments of walls incorporated in modern factories. Former manager's house, now derelict, adjacent to railway. Also slag-built chapel and attached residence. Glassworks closed 1903, became chemical works, now closed.

GLASS WASTE 518963
Gerards Bridge.

Mound of 19th century glass waste known as 'Burgy' bank (pronounced with hard 'g'). Mixture of ground glass, sand and soda, produced during glass polishing.

RAVENHEAD WINDMILL 503943
Ravenhead Road, St. Helens.

Brick tower, possibly windmill providing power for glass polishing. Adjacent a row of three cottages formerly part of Pilkington Boys Hostel, built 1916. Converted to house 1927.

MUCKY MOUNTAINS 575945
Sankey Valley Park, Earlestown.

Large mound of alkali waste from Muspratts Vitriol Works (1831-1850s) of which no buildings remain, although tall tapering octagonal chimney marked the site until 1924. Impressive waste tip illustrates movements of alkali industry from canal at St. Helens down towards Mersey at Widnes.

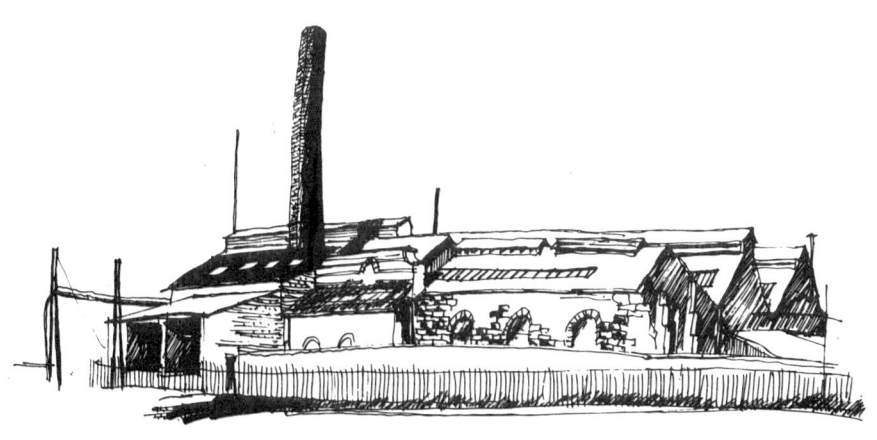

13 *Sutton Copper Works.*

COPPER WORKS - SUTTON ROLLING
MILLS   536940
Water Lane, Sutton.

Founded by William Keates in 1859, date on chimney. Oldest buildings of local stone contain two pairs of single pass rollers of considerable age. Latterly driven by electricity; building on south side probably contained beam engine. Two gas fired annealing furnaces and various pits for quenching and scale removal set in floor of cast-iron plates. Modern building houses rolling machines of various dates which are fast becoming redundant.

COPPER WORKS   537968
Stanley Bank Farm, Blackbrook.

Area of broken brick and copper slag in fields south of Stanley Bank Farm. Pewfall colliery line visible as shallow cutting, south of present farm track.

VARLEY'S IRON FOUNDRY   519956
Pocket Nook Street/Atlas Street.

Building, now dilapidated, in use as iron foundry only since 1896. Boundary wall contains numerous large blocks of copper slag from previous use as copper works. Inscriptions 'P.N.S.W. 1854' (Pocket Nook Smelting Works) over blocked doorway.

VULCAN FOUNDRY   585940
Vulcan Village, Newton-le-Willows.

Founded by Charles Tayleur in 1830 for locomotive construction. Robert Stephenson joined 1832. Extensive world-wide steam locomotive production until 1970, now Ruston Diesels. Earliest building the 1907 Institute.

HOLMAN MICHEL LEAD SMELTING
WORKS   515951
Inner Ring Road, St. Helens.

Between railway and canal. Complex of single-storey buildings of 1882, with large chimney. In use for lead smelting.

OIL AND TALLOW WORKS   523963
Islands Brow, St. Helens.

Adjacent to Sankey Canal. Chimney alone remains. Lamp oils and candles made from vegetable and animal oils. Now garage.

PAPER MILL   401053
Knowsley Road, Eccleston.

Two-storey stone building, with large loading bay and curious slit windows. In 1911, a water-powered mill, later became part of a farm.

COURISTAN CARPET FACTORY
503953
Eccleston Street, St. Helens.

A magnificently proportioned five-storey edifice with interesting arched windows. About 1890. Has also been warehouse and mill. Formerly Thornton's Rug Factory.

BEECHAM'S FACTORY   508954
Westfield Street, St. Helens.

Attractive ornamental building with distinctive clock tower of 1886. Beecham began making his famous pills in St. Helens in 1859.

CORNMILL   535968
Sankey Valley Park, Blackbrook.

19th century watermill excavated early 1980s. Foundations, with wheel pit and outbuildings. Documentary evidence of iron slitting mill in same area.

WINDLE MALT HOUSE   4765967
north of Rainford Road, Dentons Green.

Built 1777 with two storeys and two loading bays. Now a residence.

14 *Rainhill Skew Bridge, 1830.*

15 *Sankey Viaduct, 1830.*

ROAD TRANSPORT

TURNPIKE MILESTONES

Milestones were ordered to be placed on the Warrington Road in December 1753. At Rainhill Stoops (502903) is a stone of triangular section which is typical; on Rainhill railway bridge (491914) is a flat stone.

CANAL TRANSPORT

THE SANKEY CANAL

Sponsored by Common Council of Liverpool, built by Henry Berry. Nominally a navigation of the Sankey Brook; in reality, Britain's first industrial canal. Opened from Mersey to Parr in 1757, extended to Gerard's Bridge, Blackbrook Basin and Ravenhead in 1770s. Abandoned above Newton Common Lock 1932, below in 1955. North of M62 now filled and developed as linear park. Ravenhead Branch partly in water. At 512952, the "Hotties" where canal water is used for cooling. Foundations of swing bridges and stone sleeper block on the banks. New double lock, a staircase pair, under restoration at 520962. Gerard Bridge branch in water. Blackbrook branch in water, and terminal basin north of A58 is preserved. Three tramways unloaded here. Foundations of quays, turning basins, LNWR boundary cast-iron markers. Near adjacent Ship Inn, at 534957, is dock which served Pewfall colliery tramway. Old double lock (536961), oldest British example of staircase lock (two rise). Barrel-shaped in plan, preserved as cascade, no gates. Broad Oak Basin (537957) also landscaped. Three sunken abandoned Mersey Flats (typical Sankey Canal craft) found during this work, and reburied. Haydock Lock (545959) early barrel-shaped plan, half buried, gates gone. Former lock at Bradley (573944), probably best surviving on the canal. Trail leaflets produced by Sankey Valley Park.

RAIL TRANSPORT

Two working lines cross St. Helens district. The Liverpool and Manchester joined these towns in 1830 and became part of the LNWR in 1846. The LNWR line between Huyton and St. Helens opened 1871. Made connection with 1869 Lancashire Union Railway (later LNWR) to Wigan at St. Helens Shaw Street, renamed Central in 1988.

RAINHILL STATION 492914
Station Road, Rainhill.

L&MR. Present building 1860-70 replaced original which was further east. Single-storey brick, hipped slate roof, solid canopy on cast-iron columns. At west end of platform, a skew-bridge carrying Liverpool to Warrington turnpike. Most acute skew on the L&MR, of rusticated sandstone. Plaque names 'George Stephenson 1829' as engineer. Widened 1863. Eastwards the site of the Rainhill Locomotive Trials at which 'Rocket' won. Half mile west is Stoney Lane Bridge. Adjacent a chimney base, with foundation works and steps, part of boiler to provide hot water for locomotives in 1830s.

MARSHALL'S CROSS BRIDGE 519924
Marshall's Cross Road, A570.

L&MR, now bypassed. Intact and in good condition. Typical, rusticated sandstone. Compare New Street Bridge 523926, or underbridge at Lea Green 504917.

ST. HELENS JUNCTION STATION
536933
Station Road, Sutton.

L&MR, opened 1832. Present single-storey brick building 1860s by LNWR. Former bay platform for Shaw Street branch on north side. Adjacent stationmaster's house, 'Junction Inn' and railway cottages. Half mile west is St. Helens Railway overbridge, about 1833, much rebuilt. Just south of this bridge is LNWR stores building (531929) incorporating 1854 engine shed of St. Helens Railway.

SANKEY VIADUCT 568947
1 mile west of Earlestown Station.

Nine arches of 50 feet span, 60 feet high, carried L&MR over Sankey Brook and canal. Of local brick, with sandstone facings. Completed 1829, engineer George Stephenson; consultant Jesse Hartley.

EARLESTOWN STATION 578951

A triangular junction. L&MR line runs east-west. Lines west-south and east-south opened by Warrington and Newton Railway of 1832, extended to London as Grand Junction in 1837. West-south platforms disused.

In west angle is ornate sandstone building in Tudor style. Fine doorways and superb west window. Three sets of tall chimneys. Canopy on cast-iron columns to L&MR lines. Possibly built about 1840 as G.J.R. board room. On north side, a late 19th century single-storey red brick ticket office. All other platform buildings demolished. Haydock Colliery Railway formerly crossed L&MR through middle of triangle.
To west (571949), is former Viaduct Wagon Works of 1833, taken over by London and North Western Railway in 1853. Remains of later buildings incorporated in industrial estate.

Earlestown a LNWR settlement of 1850-60s. Named after Hardman Earle, director of the Company. Many houses remain to north-west of station.

NEWTON-LE-WILLOWS STATION 594954
Warrington Road, Newton.

L&MR, immediately east of impressive four-arched viaduct, a two-storey building with booking office below and waiting room above: brick, with Tudor style doors and windows, probably 1840s.

PARKSIDE STATION 605955
Lowton.

William Huskisson killed here at opening of L&MR, commemorated by contemporary Egyptian style marble monument. Staircase and foundations of station buildings visible in undergrowth, closed 1840s. Two hundred yards east is junction with Wigan Branch Railway of 1832, and site of later LNWR Parkside station closed in 1878.

ECCLESTON PARK STATION 482929
Portico Lane, Eccleston Park.

Huyton and St. Helens Railway. Single-storey wooden building, probably original 1871. Adjacent a pumphouse once supplying Sutton Oak engine shed on St Helens & Runcorn Gap Railway.

THATTO HEATH CUTTING 489933
below Elm Road, Thatto Heath.

Huyton and St. Helens Railway, 1871, a deep rock cutting rivalling Olive Mount. At south-west end is Thatto Heath Station.

ST. HELENS STATION 516953
Shaw Street, St. Helens.

Modern buildings replace LNWR structures of 1871, when Shaw Street Station replaced Raven Square and Warrington Old Road stations. Renamed Central in 1988.

Substantial LNWR brick goods shed and other buildings north of Corporation Street bridge. Station avoiding line traceable with bridge at Pocket Nook, 519957, dated 1878.

ST. HELENS AND RUNCORN GAP RAILWAY 516953 to 528915

Opened 1833 between St. Helens Raven Square and Spike Island, Widnes, as outlet for coal. Charles Vignoles, engineer. Became LNWR in 1864, now closed and lifted. Crossed L&MR on overbridge at 531930. Original narrow sandstone bridge at Baxters Lane, 526941. Remains of Sutton Oak Station 529939; Sutton Oak engine shed 526941 now a discount store.

RAINFORD BRANCH RAILWAY

Opened 1858 as northward extension of St. Helens and Runcorn Gap Railway, running north-west from Gerard's Bridge, 516964, to join LYR Liverpool-Wigan line. Trackbed converted into linear park. At Crank, a row of ornate railway cottages next to station site. Curved platforms hidden in undergrowth at Rainford Junction, nondescript LYR station buildings and signal box (478026).

ECCLESTON BRANCH

Opened 1859, survives as siding north of United Glass Works, 516948. Westwards, traces of line pass through tunnel at Greenbank, the Triplex Works (488954) and north of Eccleston Mere (482952) to the site of Gillars Green Colliery (476948). Ravenshead branch runs from Eccleston branch to serve glassworks. At 504943, remains of branch to Greengate Brickworks.

BLACKBROOK BRANCH

Can be traced from Worsley Brow via Broad Oak (531937 to 525973). Linked various collieries. Joined Lancashire Union Railway from Wigan in 1880.

COLLIERY TRAMWAYS

Several can be traced on 1848 map. Probably early 19th century, they used stone sleeper blocks, many of which remain. The 'Waggon Lane' (9548961) was a tramway linking Haydock Colliery with Sankey Canal, 1767. From Blackbrook Basin (534969) two tramways led north, embankment of one to Laffak Colliery at 529973. Other, now a footpath, passes under East Lancs Road and adjacent railway viaduct; many stone sleeper blocks built into overflow from Carr Mill Reservoir. At 553982, Blackbrook to Pewfall Colliery crosses A58; a small gatekeeper's hut survives. At Dangerous Corner, Billinge Hill, stone sleeper blocks in wall probably come from tramway serving nearby coke ovens.

PUBLIC UTILITIES

NUTGROVE GASWORKS 492724
Rainhill Road/Elton Head Road.

Small private gas works built to serve Rainhill Hospital. Exterior intact. Pre-1890 date.

WATER DAMS

Carr Mill (525980) originally supplied water to the mill. Enlarged 1826 and 1860 to provide water for Sankey Canal. Eccleston Mere (482952), built about 1860 to supply Sankey Canal. Smaller dams, possibly 18th century, at Taylor Park, Thatto Heath, Sutton Leach and adjacent to Pilkington Glass Works head offices.

WATER SUPPLY

Eccleston Lane Ends (472934), mid 19th century reservoirs now disused. Extensive underground filters exist. Small engine house and tower adjacent to St. Helens Road now contains diesel pump. Terminus of Rivington and Vyrnwy pipelines. Cast-iron valve house at end of Rivington Aqueduct adjacent to traffic lights. At Chapel Lane, Rainhill, (505907) a pumphouse on the Vyrnwy pipeline. At Sutton Oak (531937) a small building of uncertain purpose.

INDUSTRIAL HOUSING

Despite much recent demolition, there is much interesting housing throughout St. Helens. A few examples must suffice:

Factory Row (502944), a fine terrace, begun about 1784 as back-to-back houses with large end house to west. Extended eastwards and dated by plaque 1854. Railway housing at Railway Street, Pocket Nook (518957), around St. Helens Junction station and beside the former Crank Station, (502987). Colliery villages at Sutton Manor and Clock Face. Hulton Colliery houses, 1925, in Whiston and Rainhill. At Vulcan village (586938), just south of the foundry, six rows of two-storey terraced cottages dating from 1850s. At Earlestown, several mid-19th century terraced streets, part of LNWR settlement.

SEFTON

Unlike some districts of the County, Sefton does not have a previous existence as an organisational unit. The name is that of the smallest village within the area; just a 14th century church, a hall, a pub and a mill on the River Alt. It contains widely different ingredients: the former Borough of Bootle is much like Liverpool, growing out of the port with manufacturing industries following. Beyond Bootle, a number of villages have been added to the metropolitan sprawl comparatively recently. Litherland, Crosby, and later Maghull and Lydiate. A hundred years ago, these were all agricultural, now they are mainly dormitory areas. Alone in an area still rural, much of it associated with the Sefton estates and formerly the property of the Earls of Sefton, lies Formby. Beyond that, rather out on a limb both geographically and metaphorically, is Southport. This is a pleasant Victorian style seaside resort of large houses, hotels, promenades and a broad street of shops, with a slightly less salubrious hinterland usually unseen by the visitor. This heterogeneous assortment does not contain the density of interesting sites of other districts but has some items well worth a visit and others to be noted in passing.

THE PORT

For map, see page 4

THE DOCK ESTATE

The docks in Sefton are a continuation northwards of the Liverpool Dock system. To the south they are hidden behind the dock wall: to the north the Freeport and Royal Seaforth Dock can be seen through modern map of docks fencing. They are operational and permission to enter should be obtained from the Mersey Docks and Harbour Company.

BROCKLEBANK DOCK 333942

Opened as Canada Half Tide Dock in 1862, enlarged 1871, renamed 1879. Pumphouse for former Graving Dock typical of many on estate. Deteriorating common brick, pressed brick detail, iron-framed windows, wooden clerestory 1906. Chimney demolished. Steam operation until 1950s, now electric centrifugal pumps with hydraulic paddle gear.

16   *Pumphouse, Langton Dock, 1879*

LANGTON DOCK 332946

Dock opened 1879. River entrance gates are horizontal sliding curtain gates of 1962, interesting failed attempts to improve on traditional mitre gates. Superb pumphouse for the Graving Dock, one of the gems of the estate. Common brick, pressed brick detail, terracotta ornaments, stone facings and 'fairy-tale' stone tower. Datestone 1879. Dilapidated and now minus chimney and part of boiler house. Post war pumphouse at river entrance is concrete box but contains two electric and two diesel centrifugal impounding pumps to maintain water level in dock system. Derelict concrete hydraulic accumulator tower adjacent. North is Alexandra Dock of 1880, with three branches.

HORNBY DOCK 328953

Opened 1884. Former 1920s hydraulic power station (335953) is a concrete box now a workshop and store. The locomotive shed (329956) is small, typical and of brick, with adjacent lean to shed attached. MDHB locomotive No. 1 of 1906 is in care of Liverpool Museum.

GLADSTONE DOCK 334957

Opened with associated graving dock in stages from 1911 to 1927. Noted at that time for its huge size, and large enough for today's vessels. On each side at Branch Dock No.1 a three storey concrete transit shed of type once common in north docks estate, 1927.

ROYAL SEAFORTH DOCK 322964

Latest addition to Liverpool Dock system opened in 1972 with container, grain and timber terminals.

HARLAND AND WOLFF SHIP REPAIRERS 336944
Regent Road (the Dock Road), Bootle

Vaguely Renaissance two-storey office block of red brick fronts a large works complex of five bays, later extended in pressed brick. Tall semi-circular iron-framed windows and imposing doorways. About 1912, but now in poor condition. Compare Castree Brothers Packing, Strand Rd., formerly the H&W Foundry.

LIFE BOAT STATION 270063
Lifeboat Road, Formby.

Britain's oldest lifeboat station from where boats were launched prior to 1776. Red sandstone plinth and brickwork, partly buried in sand at high-water line, remain from Liverpool Corporation Dock Committee's reconstruction of 1809.

MANUFACTURING INDUSTRIES

WINDMILL 329005
Moor Lane, Great Crosby.

Early 19th century large brick tower mill, now rendered. Auxiliary steam engine 1900 and then oil engines. Disused 1960s. Now a private residence.

WINDMILL 379039
Liverpool Road, Lydiate.

Unexciting early 19th century tower mill with cement rendering incorporated into residence.

JOHNSON'S DYEWORKS 340964
Linacre Road, Bootle.

Extensive factory complex. Five-storey pressed brick unit resembling late 19th century Lancashire cotton mill. Tower boasts date 1817, making Johnson's an old established firm. Workers housing adjacent.

LIVERPOOL ELECTRIC CABLE CO. 347964
Linacre Lane, Bootle.

Extensive two-storey brick complex, with north lights roof. Iron windows. About 1912. Now 'Vactite' Advanced Cable Technology and in good order.

VULCAN ENGINEERING WORKS
373194
Rufford Road, Crossens.

1907 factory of nine bays, three-storey offices, and tower of pressed Accrington brick. Nice details.

SHRIMP BOILERS   360194
Behind houses in Marshside, Southport.

Sheds of all sorts for this traditional craft. Former shrimpers housing in Shellfield Rd. On Birkdale beach, the amphibious vehicles of the shrimper complete with Heath Robinson-ish boiling apparatus.

CANAL TRANSPORT

LEEDS AND LIVERPOOL CANAL

Liverpool to Newburgh section opened 1775. Within Sefton it is not particularly interesting or beautiful. Many locked gates; key required from British Waterways. Fixed bridges of stone, some original (e.g. Pilling Lane 366040), some erected with plaques by the Liverpool Health Authority about 1860. Swing bridges of wood (e.g. Bell's Lane 370035), still manually operated. Near Irlam Road bridge (341953) is disused small basin known as Carolina Street Wharf with gritstone paved yard and crane remnants, due for redevelopment.

RAIL TRANSPORT

Three railway routes run through Sefton. The Liverpool, Crosby and Southport Railway opened from Southport to Waterloo in 1848 and reached Tithebarn Street (Exchange) Station in 1850. This it shared with the East Lancashire Railway, whose line from Preston opened in the same year. Both were absorbed by the Lancashire and Yorkshire Railway. Two miles of the ELR/LYR joint line of 1861 connecting Southport with Wigan is also in Sefton. The Cheshire Lines Southport Extension, opened 1884, ran into the Borough at Aintree on its way to the coast at Ainsdale. It closed in 1952.

AINTREE STATION   366978
Ormskirk Road/Park Lane.

Opened by LYR in 1850. Rebuilt 1890s to cope with Grand National traffic. Small section of former extensive canopy remains, platform buildings demolished 1980s. Yellow brick (1880s) booking hall on Park Lane. Known as 'Sefton Arms' station to distinguish from CLC Aintree 'Central' of 1879 once adjacent, now demolished.

MAGHULL STATION   383171
Station Road, Maghull.

LYR, mostly original brick (1850) with notable decorative stonework and wooden canopy. Good signal box close by.

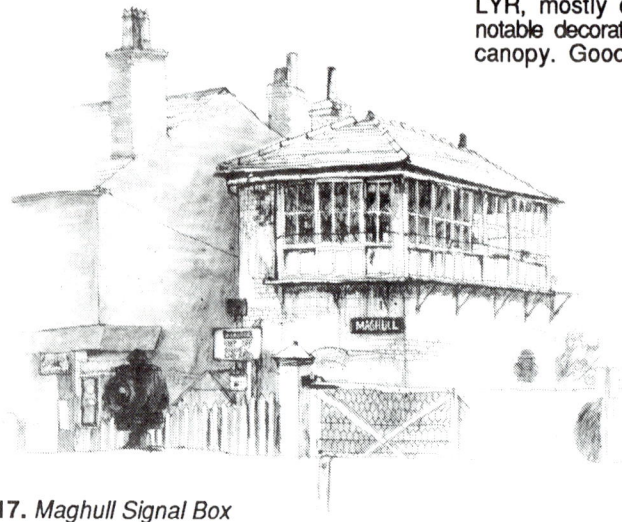

17. *Maghull Signal Box*

NEW STRAND STATION 340956
Marsh Lane, Bootle.

Opened 1850. Present platform buildings 1947 steel framed, with modular precast concrete and vitreous enamel panels. Welded steel cranked cantilever beams support minimal awnings. LMS design; first such station building in country; early BR standardisation.

HALL ROAD STATION 305006
Hall Road, Crosby.

Opened 1848. Single-storey brick offices with good details, possibly original. Fine footbridge. One-time terminus of some trains from Liverpool. Carriage sheds of modern construction on downside with traditional brick workshops to north.

FORMBY STATION 291069
Duke Street, Formby.

Opened 1848, rebuilt about 1904 with overbridge. Booking office of brick with timber roof. Fine restored LYR sign above entrance. Adjacent to the line, about one mile south, is former railway power station built for electrification in 1904. A large brick building of two bays dominating the flat countryside (295057).

FRESHFIELD STATION 291083
Victoria Road, Formby.

Level crossing, brick and timber signal box and two-storey crossing keeper's house. Compare Ainsdale Station (311122).

BIRKDALE STATION 330157
Weld Road, Southport.

Late 19th century LYR brick, with vestigial ridge and furrow awnings, subway, level crossing, signal box and staff houses. Similar to stations elsewhere on the LYR, especially in the Pennines. A good period group. Recently cleaned.

STEAMPORT 341170
Derby Road, Southport.

Brick six road LYR engine shed with fine wooden roof, erected in 1891, the home of Steamport Transport Museum. A fine collection of road and rail vehicles, many from Merseyside. Nearby is the present Chapel Street station with modern concourse and LYR glass and iron train shed.

LORD STREET STATION 331170
Lord Street, Southport.

Opened 1884 as Cheshire Lines terminus. Closed 1952; trainshed demolished, current development hopefully will retain facade. Symmetrical two-storey red brick offices, with sandstone details on three sides of concourse. Central porch under clock tower. Trackbed converted into Coastal Road to Woodvale.

PUBLIC UTILITIES

LINACRE GAS WORKS 345960
Litherland Road, Bootle.

Two old cast-iron column guided gasholders remain between four self-supporting ones. Boarded and bricked-up offices flank original main entrance of the almost cleared site.

POWER LINES 346959
over Leeds - Liverpool Canal, Bootle.

Unusual gantries carry 132kV power lines along canal for several miles in Bootle. Well seen from road bridges over canal, eg Marsh Lane (338946) and Millers Bridge (338946). Unique, early 1930s riveted shipyard construction rather than CEGB nut and bolt style. Originally built to connect former Clarence Dock power station. Currently under refurbishment.

ALTMOUTH PUMPING STATION 296044
Hightown.

Modern (1972) pumping station on River Alt. Sixty yards upstream of tidal gates (no trace remaining) built 1830 and extended 1937. System drains some 3,500 hectares and is developed from 13th century monastic and 18th century Dutch engineering work. Four diesel storm water pumps; four electric dry weather pumps.

THE PIER   330179
Southport.

First British pier designed for promenading. Erected 1859-1860, engineer James Brunlees, later of the Mersey Railway; length 3,600 feet. Extended 1864 and 1868 and later cut back. Present length 3,650 feet. Cast-iron and wood, diesel hauled 60 cm gauge railway, modern pavilions. Merseyside's other pier at New Brighton, Wirral, demolished 1973.

CONSERVATORY   336182
Hesketh Park, Southport.

A fine piece of cast-iron and glass architecture. 1860s by Edward Kemp, pupil of Sir Joseph Paxton.

SHOPS   around 340177
Lord Street, Southport.

A fine street of shops, many with ornate ironwork. Wayfarer's Arcade is especially noteworthy, 1898, architect George E. Balshaw. Good iron work also in Upper Aughton Road, Birkdale Village and Manchester Road.

PALLADIUM CINEMA   332968
Seaforth Rd./Lime Grove, Seaforth.

Small cinema built 1913 face with white glazed blocks. Symetrical front has pediment and circular window between six upright ones. Swags of fruit beneath windows in good condition produce fine effect in oblique sunshine. Now gymnasium and refrigerators.

INDUSTRIAL HOUSING

MILDMAY ROAD   around 340964
Bootle.

Two sets of late 19th century terraces, bow-fronted windows with terracotta ornament, rich in pleasing detail. Very neat and solid little houses typifying the best of what was once a wide-spread form of housing in Bootle, much of which was destroyed during the war. Close to Johnson's Dyeworks.

WIRRAL

The character of the Borough of Wirral has a simple development. Until the 19th century the area was rural and undeveloped. In 1817 the establishment of a regular steam ferry service allowed Liverpool merchants to commute across the river and build houses in the Woodside area. By the 1840s the new town of Birkenhead was growing and its main streets had been laid out. A scheme was drawn up to create docks in the tidal inlet of the Mersey known as the Wallasey Pool and the first were completed in 1847. Wallasey developed around various centres to the north of the Pool. Tramway and railway networks made commuting easy. Merchants built their houses in Oxton, West Kirby and Hoylake. New Brighton expanded to support the holiday trippers. The Mersey railway linked Wirral to Liverpool in 1886: industry came to Port Sunlight in 1888. To the east of the Borough development was slower; only in the 1920s and 1930s did settlements such as Heswall grow. Today only the mid-Wirral area around Raby and Thornton Hough retains its rural nature.

THE PORT

BIRKENHEAD DOCKS

Dock construction began in 1844 with J.M.Rendel as engineer. Morpeth and Egerton Docks were completed in 1847 south of and map connecting to the Wallasey Pool. A scheme to create a tidal basin leading into a dock made out of the Wallasey Pool was held back by financial and management problems and not properly worked on until its takeover by Liverpool Corporation in 1855. Only the creation of the MD&HB in 1858 lead to the work being restarted in earnest. The resulting Great Float of 1861 was a combination of designs from Rendel, James Abernethy, J.B. Hartley and G.F.Lyster. The tidal basin also opened but the sluicing system designed to stop it silting up was a total failure. Proper access to the Great Float was eventually provided in 1866 through the Alfred Dock and river entrances.

Disused as an entrance, the basin became Wallasey Dock in 1877 through the construction of a river wall. Morpeth was enlarged between 1868 and 1872. The Morpeth Branch Dock was built as an extension of the site old Woodside Basin and was completed in 1872. Graving docks were constructed off the West Float in 1864 and 1877. Vittoria Dock (1905) and Bidston Dock (1933) were the last docks constructed. The Great Float and Vittoria Dock remain in use, Bidston is used intermittently and Alfred provides the river entrance. Wallasey, Morpeth and Egerton Docks along with much of the land fronting the river are being developed by the Merseyside Development Corporation.

RIVER ENTRANCE 327895
Morpeth Dock.

Built 1868 in association with the Morpeth Dock extension, the massive granite walls are impressive. River lock replaced by concrete dam. Original 1847 entrance was on site of passage between Morpeth and Morpeth Branch Docks.

RIVER ENTRANCE 325903
Alfred Dock.

Hastily designed and opened in 1866 to provide access to the Great Float on the failure of the half-tide basin entrance. When built capable of taking the largest ships afloat. Three locks of differing sizes: two were combined in 1929 and filled in 1980s, one remains operational.

GATEMAN'S HUT 328892
Shore Road, Birkenhead.

Shore Road formerly a private MDHB road reached through a double gate from Woodside. The central gateman's hut is of stone and dated 1866. Inside the estate are a number of single-storey brick gate/lock keeper's huts of similar date but differing designs.

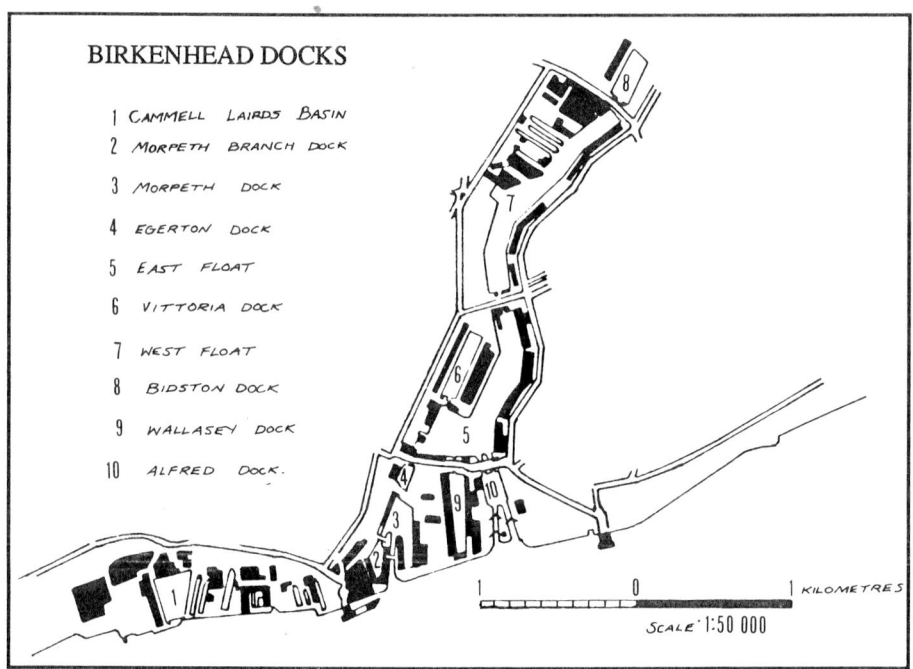

Map of Birkenhead Docks

ROAD BRIDGES
Poulton Bridge   300909
Duke Street Bridge   312902
Egerton Bridge   323896

Poulton bridge was the last swing-bridge installed. Two others are rolling counterweight lift-bridges of the Scherzer type, constructed of steel with wooden control rooms above the road. Built in the early 1930s, they replaced swing-bridges. Formerly operated by the dock hydraulic system they now operate electrically.

ROAD BRIDGES   322899
Tower Road, Birkenhead.

Known as 'The Four Bridges' these have been upgraded during 1989. From north to south: the still working 1930s rolling counterweight lift-bridge and a modern roadway replacing former swing-bridge over Alfred Dock, fixed former lift-bridge over Wallasey Dock and modern roadway over Egerton Dock.

HYDRAULIC GENERATING STATION
                          322899
Tower Road, Birkenhead.

Designed by J.B.Hartley, son of Jesse Hartley. Built 1863 to provide power for lock gates and bridges of Birkenhead Dock system. Brick castellated tower with stone facings remains impressive despite being foreshortened by war damage. Brick engine house also rebuilt and now used as engineers store.

HYDRAULIC ACCUMULATOR TOWER
                          325902
Alfred Dock river entrance.

Square brick castellated tower of 1866. Unusually squat because much of shaft is below ground level. Built up hydraulic power lost in transmission from Tower Road generator to operate the six lock gates of the three Alfred river entrances.

PUMPING STATION 327899
Wallasey Dock.

Built 1890 to maintain artificially high water levels in Dock system in order to allow access for deeper draughted vessels. The river water was pumped into Wallasey Dock where it deposited its silt and eventually made the dock unusable. Red brick and terracotta engine house, slate roof and arched windows. Original vertical steam engines and pumps abandoned 1955 and removed 1980s. Adjacent 1955 block contained Gwynne steam turbines and pumps. Turbines replaced by one diesel and three electric motors in mid-1980s. Original boiler house and chimney. Boilers possibly unique in being suspended.

WOODSIDE LAIRAGE 329893
Shore Road, Birkenhead.

Between Woodside and Morpeth Branch Dock were offices, slaughterhouses, meat stores and one of the earliest chill room (refrigerated) complexes in the country. Opened in 1879, soon making Birkenhead the most important port after London for the import of livestock. Offices remain, much else lost to redevelopment in 1990 as a business park.

CATTLE LANDING STAGE 328898
Morpeth / Wallasey river wall.

Three landward piers of the Wallasey landing stage remain. Iron pillars date from 1876, northernmost wooden pillars date from 1900 extension. Stage removed 1966-7. Cattle walkway from here to Wallasey and Woodside lairages now largely demolished. Sections remain in front of Tunnel ventilation tower and along northern shed of Morpeth Branch dock. Some iron pillars remain of former walkway swingbridge over Morpeth entrance.

ONE O'CLOCK GUN EMPLACEMENT
328896
River Wall, Morpeth Dock.

Site of the one o'clock gun fired by electric signal from Bidston Observatory to transmit time to vessels in the river. Original red brick and sandstone hut of 1868 altered in 1930s by addition of concrete and brick second storey.

SLUICE CONTROL HOUSES 322899
Tower Road, Birkenhead.

Located each side of passage between Wallasey Dock and East Float, two long low brick sheds of 1863. Housed machinery to open and close sluice gates controlling release of water from Great Float to scour silt from Wallasey Dock, at that time a tidal basin. Scheme failed, machinery removed and houses reused.

WAREHOUSE 327892
Shore Road, Birkenhead.

Typical Cheshire Lines Committee rail connected warehouse of common brick. Curved facade, impressive doorways, original signs, built 1871. Extended 1890s in red brick, with cast-iron windows to Canning Street. Now Littlewoods.

CORN WAREHOUSES 316904
Dock Road, Wallasey.

Three warehouses built by MDHB engineer G.F. Lyster in 1868, of which parts remain. Six-storeys of brick, with heavily moulded windows and doors. Hoists. An arm of the dock ran between to facilitate the unloading of mainly American grain. 20th century warehouses adjacent.

Immediately west are the massive mills built 1893 to 1914. Spillers Homepride, formerly Paul Bros (1902) contains roller mills of early date. To north of dock road is Buchanans of 1893.

STONE SHED 328894
Pacific Road/ Morpeth Branch Dock.

Transit shed of 1872 in standard pattern but uniquely constructed of rubble sandstone instead of the usual brick. Due for development as transport museum for Wirral Borough Council.

LNWR SHED 322895
Egerton Dock.

Warehouse built in LNWR pattern in red and blue bricks, adjacent to site of former goods yard. Originally three storey with stage extension over the dock. Close by, the signal box, level crossing and footbridge at Canning Street form a nice group.

FERRY LANDING STAGE 329892
Woodside, Birkenhead.

Town of Birkenhead purchased ferry rights in 1858. Present landing stage of steel and plastic opened 1985 to replace original of 1861. Original large airy booking hall of wood and cast-iron remains, now a visitor centre with preserved booking kiosks, historic notices and other relics. Rebuilt part of earlier 1835 jetty visible with stump of lighthouse.

FERRY LANDING STAGE 326908
Seacombe, Wallasey.

Original jetty replaced in 19th century and again in 1933. Building is brick with stone detailing, in typical art deco style of the period. Good clock tower, windows and spacious interior with ticket offices. Headquarters of ferry operations.

FERRY TICKET OFFICE 356818
Eastham Woods Country Park, Ferry Road, Eastham.

Single-storey sandstone building with datestone 'Eastham Ferry 1856'. River elevation has bay window overlooking landing stage abutment. Saved from demolition by NWSIAH and now a public toilet. Ferries to Liverpool suspended 1929, stage removed 1935. 'Jobs's Ferry' 200 yards downstream had served the first steam ferries in 1816.

ROCK FERRY PIER 336869
Bedford Road, Rock Ferry.

Sandstone pier remains; overshadowed by modern steel jetties of Tranmere oil terminal. 18th century ferry terminal, greatly improved by Royal Rock Ferry Company in 1834. Parts of Esplanade, Bath Houses and Hotel remain. Adjacent is Rock Park, quality merchants housing of similar date. Ferry closed 1939.

Landward abutments of Egremont and New Ferry jetties remain. Part of Monks Ferry visible under MDC redevelopment.

SEA DEFENCES 260918
Moreton.

Wallasey Embankment, two miles long built in 1829 to prevent flooding. Heavily rebuilt.

FORT AND LIGHTHOUSE 309947
Perch Rock, New Brighton.

Fort built 1826-9 by Royal Engineers to defend the Mersey estuary. Designed by Capt. John Kitson. Reached by causeway at low tide. Runcorn sandstone, with four round corner towers and impressive landward entrance. Extensive alterations in 1890s removed two seaward towers. Remaining pair given concrete observation posts 1941. Barracks, magazines, batteries and parade grounds remain inside. Open to the public. Lighthouse of Anglesey granite built 1827-30 on site of wooden marker 'perch' by John Foster, the Liverpool Corporation Surveyor.

LEASOWE LIGHTHOUSE   253914
Pasture Road/Leasowe Road, Moreton.

First Mersey lighthouses built in 1760s, two at Leasowe and two at Hoylake. This, the upper Leasowe light, a white circular brick structure 101 feet high tapering towards top. Walls several feet thick, seven storeys, uppermost having gallery facing N.W. Datestone above doors reads "M.W.G. 1763" referring to William Gregson, Mayor of Liverpool. Considerable rebuilding 1824 included insertion of cast-iron staircase. Original light a coal fire; three oil burners and reflector installed 1722. Last used 1908, then a cafe, then derelict, recently rehabilitated by Wirral Borough Council.

LIGHTHOUSE   300099
Bidston Hill, Birkenhead.

Built 1873 by Mersey Docks and Harbour Board to replace earlier structure of 1771. Three storeys of stone, with lamp room above and keeper's house adjacent. Last used 1913.

Adjoining is the former MDHB Observatory built 1860s for time keeping and tide prediction. Fired a gun electrically at Morpeth Dock as one o' clock time signal. Telescope and prediction machines in care of Liverpool Museum. Both in grounds of Natural Environment Research Council laboratories.

To south a series of holes in the sandstone, bases for flagpoles of pre-electric telegraph system announcing arrival of vessels off Holyhead.

UPPER LIGHTHOUSE   215892
Valentia Road, Hoylake.

Octagonal brick building of 1865 now a private residence. Last used 1886.

GRANGE BEACON   223866
Column Road, West Kirby.

Tall sandstone column erected 1841 by Trustees of Liverpool Docks as landmark for shipping. On site of Grange Mill.

18. *Leasowe Lighthouse*

MINING AND QUARRYING

STORETON QUARRY 313845
off Mount Road, Higher Bebington.

Probably worked from Roman times. Provided stone for Hamilton Square (1830-40), the original Philharmonic Hall, Liverpool, (1845) and many other buildings on both sides of the Mersey. Filled with spoil from Mersey Road Tunnel, 1926-31. Little visible today, but line of Tramway can be traced in Storeton Woods as embankment and tunnel portals under Mount Road. Reused stone sleeper blocks at Rest Hill Road/Mount Road 314846, also bridge carrying Birkenhead Railway over tramway at 336839. Tramway rail came secondhand from Liverpool and Manchester Railway in 1836. Other quarries at Heswall and Lower Tranmere.

MANUFACTURING INDUSTRIES

VAUXHALL IRON FOUNDRY 301902
Beaufort Road, Birkenhead.

Early 19th century brick foundry hall now cement rendered. Cast-iron arched windows now bricked up. Dominant roof ventilators. Formerly on the shore of the Wallasey Pool, said to be John Laird's original works of 1824, from which he launched his first iron ship in 1829.

CAMMELL LAIRDS SHIPBUILDING YARD
329882
New Chester Road, Birkenhead.

Lairds moved here about 1858 from old works on Wallasey Pool. Four graving docks of the 1860s remain. After Laird Bros. amalgamated with Charles Cammell and Company in 1903, yard extended southwards, including new wide fitting-out basin, to cover 108 acres. Pioneered both iron and steel ship construction. Many famous vessels constructed here including the Alabama, two Ark Royals and Mauritania II. Current work mainly naval; access restricted.

CANADA WORKS 301901
Beaufort Road, Birkenhead.

Curtain wall and scanty remains only of 1853 Peto and Brassey's iron founding, locomotive and ship building works. Supplied ironwork, bridges and locomotives for Canada's Grand Trunk Railway. Two of the three graving docks now filled. Nearby the Grand Trunk pub.

ENGINEERING, BOILERMAKING, IRON
AND BRASS FOUNDRY 320894
Marcus Street, Birkenhead.

Gordon Allison's foundry. Three extensive ranges of common brick. Two-storey curved brick frontage about 1875, now workshop units.

BIDSTON WINDMILL 287894
Vyner Road, Birkenhead.

Tower mill 1790s, disused 1870s. Restored 1894 and preserved by Corporation since 1920s. Brick rendered over, 29 feet high, 19 feet diameter at base, tapering to top. Wooden 1927 replacement cap of upturned boat shape. Common sails with leading boards. (1927) to cast-iron cross on iron wind shaft. Original brakewheel missing, present brake modern in design. Two pairs of French stones on first floor, governors and much other drive gear remaining. Entry to interior controlled by Dept. of Leisure Services, Wirral Borough Council.

Site of earlier post mill, 150 feet to north, with marks of cross trees and parts of circle worn by tail-pole still visible.

19. *Bidston Windmill*

FLOUR MILLS 304902
off Beaufort Street, Birkenhead.

Huge flour mill on the West Float built by Joseph Rank Ltd. in 1912. Massive red brick multi-storey block, grainstores and offices. Others followed by Spillers (1914), and Vernon and Sons (1898).

TANNERY 326878
New Chester Road, Birkenhead.

British Leather Company's brick multi-storey works built in 1906. On site of earlier tanning yards built on what was river bank about 1878.

BIRKENHEAD BREWERY 314883
Oxton Road, Birkenhead.

Mid 19th century brick building with rusticated stone facings and glazed clerestory roof. Cement rendered: now a motor-bike shop. Opposite, the bottling plant.

LEVER BROS. FACTORY 337829
Wood Street, Port Sunlight.

William Hesketh Lever started soap works 1888. Curtain wall only of No. 1 soapery dated 1888/1893. Ornamental stone front of No. 2 soapery 1893, extended in brick, both in Wood Street. Other extensions 1913-14 and later behind.

WINDMILL 277813
Telegraph Road, Gayton, Heswall.

Circular sandstone tower mill. Two-storeys. Built about 1760, last used 1875, now a dwelling.

VILLAGE SMITHY 303809
Thornton Hough.

One of the last smithies in the borough, where the old craft is still practised. Built 1905.

ROAD TRANSPORT

MERSEY TUNNEL ENTRANCE 326887
King's Square, Birkenhead.

Tunnelling 1925-1934. Architecture 1931-34, now much altered. Engineers Sir Basil Mott and J.M. Brodie. Architect A.L. Rowse. Port-land stone, entrance lodges, art deco detailing. 60 foot black granite column remains, although moved. Secondary 'Dock entrance' in Rendel Street, 320894, disused and less altered.

MERSEY TUNNEL VENTILATION STATION 329893
Pacific Road, Birkenhead.

Monolithic brick block with stone details, 210 feet high, dominating riverside. Two exhaust and four blowing fans for mid-river ventilation. Smaller similar towers at Sidney Street (325892) for main tunnel and Taylor Street (322892) for the dock branch.

POULTON BRIDGE 337816
Dibbinsdale Road, Bromborough.

Single sandstone arched bridge 1835. Rebuilt and widened 1980.

LEVER CAUSEWAY 310853
Higher Bebington - Storeton.

An example of Lord Leverhulme's private roads, originally leading to Thornton Hall. 1912-1914.

TOLL BAR COTTAGE 282809
Chester High Road, Gayton, Heswall.

Single-storey cottage, about 1825. Crudely patched 1970s. Now abandoned, and roofless.

MILESTONE 283808
100 yards south of Toll Bar Cottage.

Cast iron, 1896, by Cheshire County Council, a typical example. Compare 282822 or 248843. Cast iron finger signposts of similar date at Eastham village, Heswall traffic lights and elsewhere.

PAINTED FENCES 318804
B5151 at Four Lanes End.

Black and white painted fence at road junctions a Cheshire County Council safety feature. Early 20th century. Also at 319814.

TRAM DEPOT 306880
Palm Grove, Oxton, Birkenhead.

Britain's first street tramway opened between Woodside and the Park Entrance on the instigation of George Train in 1860. Line extended to Palm Grove and depot and stables established in the following year. 1879 office building of Birkenhead Tramways Company remains: yard and buildings to rear much altered.

TRAM DEPOT 304898
Laird Street, Birkenhead.

Birkenhead Corporation built this depot for its new electric trams in 1900-01. Brick offices front extensive sheds and workshops.

First buses 1918, last trams 1937, now Merseybus garage.

CANAL TRANSPORT

EASTHAM LOCKS 370810
off Ferry Road, Eastham.

First mile of Manchester Ship Canal is in Merseyside. Opened 1894, last canal in Britain. Engineer Sir Edward Leader Williams. Three sea locks at Eastham 600 x 80 feet, 350 x 50 feet, 150 x 30 feet (the last disused). Adjacent Queen Elizabeth II oil dock with its own entrance lock opened 1954.

RAIL TRANSPORT

The Chester and Birkenhead opened 1840 and became London and North Western and Great Western Joint in 1860. Hoylake Railway opened 1866, extended as Wirral Railway to West Kirby and New Brighton in 1880s. Seacombe branch (1895) now Wallasey road tunnel approach. Wrexham, Mold and Connah's Quay, later Great Central, joined Wirral at Bidston 1896. Mersey Railway, 1886 with steam traction, 1903 with electric, joined Wirral Railway to Liverpool. Trackbed and preserved Hadlow Road Station remain on Hooton to West Kirby line, opened throughout 1886.

GRANGE LANE STATION 326887
Borough Road East, near Mersey Road tunnel approach, Birkenhead.

Facade of original 1840 Chester & Birkenhead Railway terminus supports advertisement hoarding. Closed 1844 when Town station on new Monks Ferry branch opened in adjacent and now derelict semi-filled cutting. Entrances to Monks Ferry and Woodside (1878) tunnels just visible. Town closed 1945.

SPITAL STATION 339831
Spital Road, Bebington.

Red brick, half timbered gables. LNWR & GWR rebuild of 1893. Platform structures demolished. Compare with Bebington (platform shelter remains) and Bromborough.

NORTH STATION 298903
Station Road, Birkenhead.

No remains of original 'Docks' station opened by Hoylake Railway in 1866. Present building 1881-1891 to standard Wirral Railway design. Compare with Wallasey Grove Road and New Brighton. Red brick, terracotta details, sandstone windows and slate roof. Offices and stationmaster's house at each end, covered waiting area between. Carved sandstone Wirral horn on gables. Overbridge, iron and wood canopy on island up platforms.

No. 1 signal box on down platform. No. 2 signal box adjacent to nearby seven road carriage shed rebuilt after war damage and recently extended.

BIDSTON STATION 284908
School Lane, Bidston.

Opened 1866. Present lonely single island platform with wooden buildings 1896, with adjacent Dee Junction signal box controlling GCR line to Wrexham. Extensive GCR Bidston yards now all gone.

HOYLAKE STATION 216888
Station Road, Hoylake.

Opened 1866 as terminus of Hoylake Railway. Present building 1938, art deco brick and concrete with iron window-frames. Dramatic cantilevered canopy. Compare Manor Road, Meols, Moreton, Leasowe or London Transport of similar date.

WEST KIRBY STATION 213869
Grange Road, West Kirby.

Built 1896 when original single line of 1878 was doubled. Red brick booking hall and offices with imposing clock tower across end of tracks. Concourse canopy 1896, single island platform canopy of 1938. 1980s brick box booking office: original building now shops.

NEW BRIGHTON STATION 304939
Atherton Street, New Brighton.

Opened 1888. Standard Wirral Railway style. High half-panelled booking hall flanked by symmetrical stationmaster's house and offices to cope with seaside resort traffic. Across end of tracks of single island platform, canopy renewed 1938. Three stable roads. Original Wirral Rly signal box.

CENTRAL STATION 323874
Argyle Street South, Birkenhead.

Main station of the Mersey Railway, 1886. Extensive brick booking hall at street level with street canopy. Stationmaster's house and Company office adjacent. Recently cleaned. Platforms in cutting, two through lines and little used down bay. Overbridge, wooden canopies, windbreaks and tiny up-side waiting room. Three road carriage shed adjacent. Signal box. Fine Victorian atmosphere. Locomotive 'Cecil Raikes' preserved at Steamport Transport Museum, Southport.

GREEN LANE STATION 325878
Green Lane, Birkenhead.

Mersey Railway 1886. Recently cleaned brick and terracotta station and stationmaster's house. Large panelled and tiled booking hall. Platforms in stone cutting, half roofed over by steel girders and brick arches supporting LNWR and GWR Joint line to Woodside.

HAMILTON SQUARE STATION 326891
Hamilton Street, Birkenhead.

Mersey Railway 1886. Platforms 103 feet below street level, recently modernised. Original hydraulic lifts replaced by electric in 1940s and 1990. Station building in red brick and terracotta, with arched windows and airy booking hall lit by roof lights. Dominated by tall crenallated hydraulic header tower in style of Italian campanile. Original Liverpool James Street station was similar. Architect G.E. Grayson.

PUMPING STATION 328892
Shore Road, Woodside, Birkenhead.

Mersey Railway 1886. Average flow of water into tunnel 4000 gallons per minute. Impressive pumping station of common brick, with terracotta arcading. Three-storeys, with low extension to west and slate roof. Inside originally, a Hathorn Davey horizontal steam engine driving a 30 inch pump and two Barclay compound grasshopper beam engines. These drove 40 inch pumps and ran continuously until

1926 when electric pumps were introduced. Remained as standby engines until 1959 when one removed. The building cleaned and refurbished as museum 1989 with remaining Barclay as centrepiece. The 270 foot boilerhouse chimney once highest on Birkenhead riverside demolished along with adjacent 1903 MR power station in 1940.

20. *Mersey Railway Pumping Engine*

PARK STATION 310895
Duke Street, Birkenhead.

Brick booking hall on overbridge rebuilt after war damage. Two island platforms, one modernised, one disused but with original wooden waiting sheds and canopy of 1888. Spandrils show M.T.R. (Mersey Tunnel Railway) and W.M.R. (Wirral and Mersey Railways); station jointly managed. Through running before Mersey electrified in 1903, interchange until 1838, when Wirral electrified and through running resumed.

PUBLIC UTILITIES

FLAYBRICK HILL WATERWORKS 294890
Bidston Road/Upton Road, Birkenhead.

Impressive circular sandstone tower supporting iron water tank. Tower formerly housed pair of beam engines. Tower, wells, and adjacent reservoir built 1860-65 by Birkenhead Improvement Commissioners, designed by J.F. Bateman. Other water towers at Tower Road, Prenton, 1859 rebuilt 1920s, (309861); Mill Lane, Liscard, 1861, (306917); Gorse Hill, New Brighton, 1905, (303935) and Tower Road North, Heswall, 1886, (267824).

PUMPING STATION 314875
Column Road, West Kirby.

Former stone built pumping station for Hoylake & West Kirby Gas & Water Company.

PUBLIC BATHS 322914
Riverview Road, Seacombe.

Guinea Gap baths were typical municipal swimming baths, built 1908 in undistinguished red brick. Overlooking the Mersey, river water was originally used. Recently cleaned and rebuilt internally.

PILLAR BOX 309880
Balls Road/Slatey Road, Birkenhead.

Fluted pillar box, with vertical slot, cast by Smith and Hawkes of Birmingham about 1857. Installed 1981 after twelve years in adjacent Williamson Art Gallery and Museum. Hexagonal 'Penfold' boxes at Lorne Road (304880) and Ashville Road (307891).

POWER STATION 314888
Bentinck Street, Birkenhead.

Birkenhead Corporation's first 'Electricity Generating Station', built 1895, two storeys offices and power hall in red brick with terracotta detail. Extended with datestone 'Electric Lighting Station 1902' and town arms. Separate power station in adjacent Craven Street for tramways, 1901.

POWER STATION 306906
Limekiln Lane, Wallasey.

Large derelict power halls of brick and terracotta, 1915 with 1924 extension. Machinery removed.

INDUSTRIAL HOUSING

PRICE'S VILLAGE 349842
Bromborough Road.

One of the country's earliest model villages, built by Price's Patent Candle Company in 1853. Small brick-built terraced houses of different sizes in neatly laid-out streets. Managers' houses around the green. Village church, school, hall and hospital. Much recent demolition.

PORT SUNLIGHT VILLAGE 328845

W.H. Lever began his soap works and workers' housing in 1888. 28 houses built by 1890. Palatial in comparison with slums or ordinary dwellings of Birkenhead or Liverpool. House groups, wide roads and gardens emphasise spaciousness. House groups by different architects creating English village atmosphere. Much use of half-timbering and pressed red brick. Last houses built 1930s. Village now covers 140 acres. Community buildings, church, pub, village hall, Lady Lever Gallery and railway station harmonise to preserve atmosphere. Not earliest model village but surpasses all in architecture and aesthetic concept.

THORNTON HOUGH VILLAGE
305810

A complete English manorial village of brick and half-timbered cottages in many styles. Two churches, pub, village green, smithy (still working) and school. Built by first Viscount Leverhulme in 1890s for his estate workers.

21. *Port Sunlight Village*

NORTH WESTERN SOCIETY FOR INDUSTRIAL ARCHAEOLOGY AND HISTORY

The Society was founded in 1964. It runs a programme of monthly indoor lecture meetings and outdoor field visits. A regular newsletter keeps members in touch and an Journal is produced to provide an outlet for the results of fieldwork. Its members have investigated areas of dockland for the Liverpool Museum and excavated the Edge Hill terminus of the industrial Liverpool and Manchester Railway. The remains of saltworks at Hale Bank, Speke are currently being researched. The Society is represented on the Liverpool Heritage Bureau and is frequently invited to comment on planning applications and proposed developments around the region.

Details about the Society are available from the Honorary Secretary, c/o National Museums & Galleries on Merseyside, 127 Dale Street, Liverpool, L69 3LA.